Kensington Palace
essential tales

Kensington Palace
essential tales

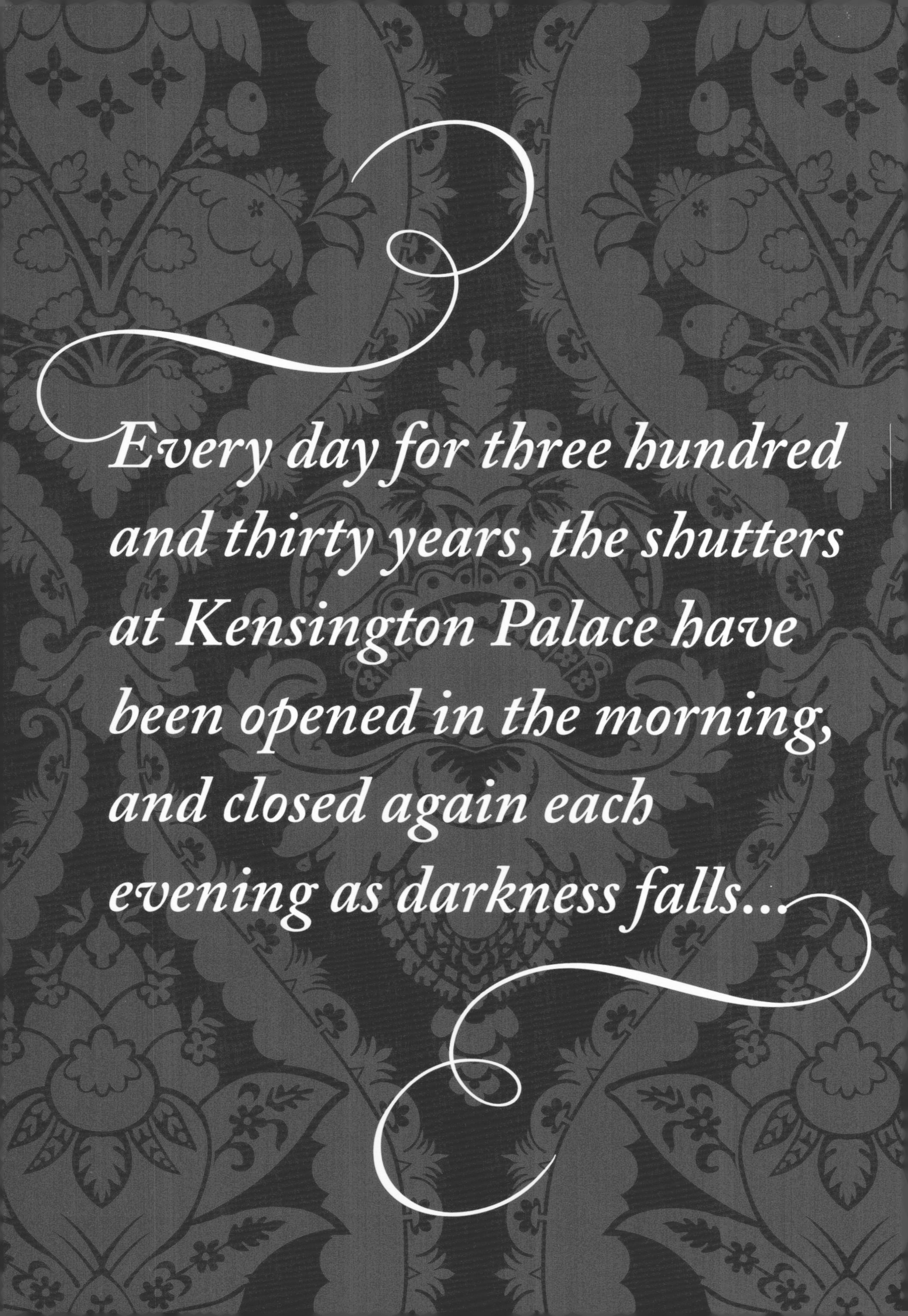
Every day for three hundred
and thirty years, the shutters
at Kensington Palace have
been opened in the morning,
and closed again each
evening as darkness falls...

1

The story of the palace

Every day for three hundred and thirty years, the shutters at Kensington Palace have been opened in the morning, and closed again each evening as darkness falls.

Though the kings and queens have long since departed, a whole community continues to protect the palace and the precious memories that echo through its great rooms. Kensington has been many things in its history: a home for families, both great and humble; a stage for the long, drawn-out drama of the nation's history; an art gallery and a museum;

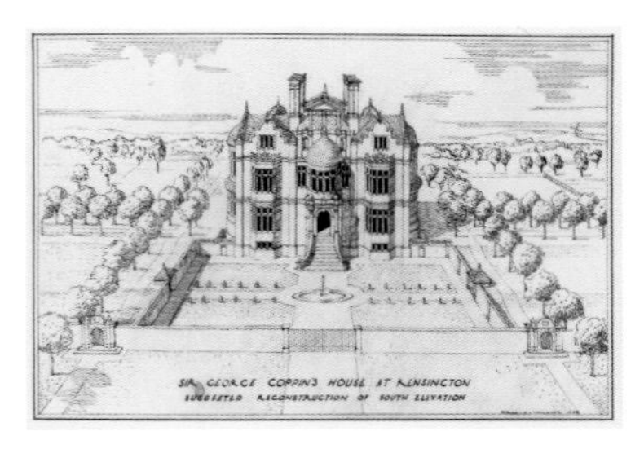

Above This modern reconstruction by Patrick Faulkner shows the south side of 'modest' Nottingham House, perhaps as William and Mary first saw it when they were house-hunting in 1689.

Right The north side of 'the King's House' at Kensington, engraved by Sutton Nicholls while the transformation was taking place, sometime between 1689 and Queen Mary's death in 1694.

but most of all a venue where history was made. For this is a place layered deeply with stories of life, love, happiness and tragedy in equal measure across the spectrum of human emotion.

In the year of Protestant triumph and revolution that was 1689, the new sovereigns William and Mary selected a modest mansion called Nottingham House to be their new home. It lay a few miles from the bustle of London, where the air was clean and fine views could be had all the way into Surrey. Sir Christopher Wren drew up plans, but the Queen herself took charge of the project to transform this house into the palace of Kensington, and set to work with excitement and hope. Even while the workmen were constructing walls, hewing the great timbers for the roofs and floors, plastering, glazing the many windows, lighting fires to air and dry the new rooms and moving earth around the gardens to create banks and parterres, designers were preparing schemes for the new rooms – panelling, carving, furnishings, textiles, mirrors, porcelain and rugs. Yet this was to be no great monumental symbol of royal vanity and power, but an intimate retreat and a cosy home for a devoted couple, just as people build today. In some ways, the palace is a testimony of a brief and promising life cut short, for Mary, contracting smallpox, died here in 1694 at the age of just 32, before the paint was barely dry.

Despite his grief, King William finished the building with a grand gallery range that the visitor approaches today, past the statue of him placed there a hundred years ago. His death in 1702 was followed by the short, eventful reign of Queen Anne. She flitted from place to place and spent

Below A mid 18th-century view of Kensington Palace by an unknown artist. Within a few years, George II would be dead and no reigning monarch would sleep within the palace for almost 70 years.

little time at Kensington, but her one extravagant gesture here is without a doubt the most beautiful orangery in the world. When it was finished in 1705 it was probably also the most expensive. Anne's death at Kensington in 1714 could have spelled the end of the palace, but the new King, George I – Georg Ludwig, Elector of Hanover – walked around it as soon as he arrived, and pronounced (in German, as he spoke poor English) that it was very agreeable, so beginning almost half a century of favour and prominence.

Strong women have always featured high in the palace's history. First came the clever Stuart sisters Mary II and Anne, and Anne's childhood friend and favourite Sarah Churchill, a wily and skilful courtier. Then there was the mistress of King George I, known disrespectfully as the Maypole or the Scarecrow; evidently she was thin, and that rankled in some quarters. George I may not have had good taste in women but under his patronage, the palace was adorned and enlarged by the artist and architect William Kent, filled with art and fine furniture and given a refined 18th-century appearance, which many of its grand rooms retain to the present day. The succession of George II and Queen Caroline in 1727 invigorated the Court; that essential mechanism of patronage, fashion, manners and society. The King and Queen could not have been more different. Caroline kept tigers in the gardens, while the King remained content with snails and tortoises. He was a boor to her sharp and enquiring mind, off campaigning while Caroline reorganised the gardens, created a cabinet of curiosities and discovered rare and precious treasures in secret closets. Yet they formed a good team, hosting lavish receptions and leading society with sparkle.

There are two ways of looking at the Court in the 18th century. On the one hand it could be seen as a collection of shimmering nobles; both men and women bewigged and bedizened, sporting embroidered silk, lace, powdered wigs and diamonds in equal measure, where entry to the palace was measured in terms of how you dressed and even a common tart could sweep up the King's Grand Staircase and gain access to the throne according to the cut of her cloth. On the other hand we have Horace Walpole's description of a creeping malaise which gradually gripped the palace after the early death of Queen Caroline in 1737; the King's mistresses ageing disgracefully, endless games of cards, the same dreary gossip shunted back and forth and the shuffling of faded silk dresses on the oak floors. These old courtiers, he said, were like flies in the autumn, sunning themselves at a window, past even buzzing, and waiting for the hurricane of a new reign to sweep them all away. That tempest was to come in October 1760, when the King fell dead in his privy closet at Kensington one morning. No reigning monarch would sleep within the palace walls for almost 70 years, and for an age the great

chambers lay silent and neglected. For a shilling the curious tourist could tip the housekeeper and, by the light of a candle, peer at the gloomy paintings and lift the dust sheets on the gilded furnishings. The position of Kensington at the epicentre of society was evidently over, and it is little wonder that the damp set in and the palace became populated by a rag-bag of minor royals and hangers-on.

If we forward our story to the year 1819, we return to Kensington at the conclusion of a desperate race. In that year, George III, supposedly mad and locked away at Windsor for a whole decade, was dying. Despite his dutiful and prolific production of 15 children, no direct heir had survived and it looked like the Hanoverian dynasty might fail. In May, his fourth son, the Duke of Kent, and his heavily pregnant wife sped on carriages overland through Germany, took the fast packet boat to England and raced on to London in an effort to make sure the child would be born on English soil, and preferably in a royal palace. The duchess arrived in the nick of time, to give birth to a healthy girl. A few days later, the State Apartments came back to life – briefly – as Princess Alexandrina Victoria was baptised in a huge gilded wine cooler in the splendour of the Cupola Room. Eighteen years later, after a formative education spent almost entirely within the confines of the palace, the young princess was woken early by unexpected visitors to learn that the mantle of destiny had fallen on her young shoulders. The Victorian age began at Kensington.

Kensington in the 19th century took on a new life as a haunt of eccentrics and a royal dormitory. Queen Victoria's uncle Augustus, Duke of Sussex was a long-term resident, manically collecting books which he stored in every nook and cranny. Wearing his banyan and cap, visitors recounted that as he moved from room to room, he would be followed by a flapping menagerie of small dogs and birds, with his tiny wife bringing up the rear. Later in the century, more royals arrived; among them were the diminutive Francis, Duke of Teck and his over-sized wife Mary Adelaide who had to scurry away to Florence in 1883 to avoid their creditors. Their daughter Victoria May would in time marry the heir to the throne and become Queen Mary, one of the most loyal advocates and friends of the palace. Queen Victoria also lodged two of her daughters in the palace; Princess Louise, a talented and gifted artist in her own right, and her serious, younger sister Princess Beatrice. As they aged and an even younger generation grew up, the palace became known as the 'the aunt heap'.

In a palace where time might stand still, change is in fact constant. In 1898 the doors to the State Apartments were thrown open to the public and the palace became the repository of London's history; its galleries and rooms were cluttered with display cases – but only briefly, as Suffragette

Previous page The King's Drawing Room in 1819, transformed by George III for his fourth son, Edward, Duke of Kent. These are the rooms that the Duke's daughter Victoria, later Queen Victoria, would have known, where she lived and played as a girl. Engraved by W J Bennett from W H Pyne's *The History of the Royal Residences*, 1819.

Below The south front of Kensington Palace today, with the statue of William III presented to Edward VII in 1907 by the King's nephew, Kaiser William II.

threats forced its closure. The Luftwaffe dropped incendiaries in 1940, making two princesses homeless, but ever resilient and no doubt well built, the palace survived to be cherished by a new generation. The old Victorian princesses departed and a new generation took centre stage. Princess Margaret hosted a miniature court of pop stars and artists in the 1960s, while a grand apartment built for an 18th-century Prince of Wales became a refuge and home for his late 20th-century counterpart. Fame and focus descended on the building in more tragic circumstances in 1997, with the death of the People's Princess and few can forget the sea of flowers and the solemn departure of the funeral cortège for Diana, Princess of Wales. Life and death have been a constant theme at Kensington and the cycle continues. We are all, high and low, but passing visitors, and if we are lucky, we too may become part of its incredible story.

2

The King who loved too much

It was a bright morning at Kensington Palace in spring 1694 and a special birthday treat had been arranged for Queen Mary II. In front of the palace, the commander surveyed his troops with pride, arranged in neat lines on the palace lawns. All stood stiffly to attention, waiting for the order to parade before the Queen. This was also an opportunity for the head of the army, King William III, to review the troops.

Impressed by this pleasing display of loyalty, and the enthusiastic playing of the companies' drummers, the King rewarded the troops with 20 gold guineas. Yet the King had no intention of using these soldiers in battle, for the two companies were merely boys, armed with wooden muskets and swords, and their commander was his nephew, five-year-old William, Duke of Gloucester.

Above William III by Sir Peter Lely, 1677. William was a skilled solider; a dashing figure to his young nephew (right) who admired him greatly.

Opposite William, Duke of Gloucester by Edmund Lilly, 1698. Here in his ninth year, the young boy already cut an impressive figure, and embodied his uncle's hopes as his chosen heir. Sadly, it was not to be.

William and Mary had no children of their own, but they both adored their nephew. He was the son of the Queen's sister, Princess Anne, and her husband Prince George of Denmark, born on 24 July 1689 and named after the King. He was doubly precious as the only one of Anne's many children to survive beyond birth and infancy. However, William Henry was a sickly child, and his regular bouts of illness were a terrible worry. The family moved to Campden House in Kensington, less than a mile from the palace, in the hope that the country air would be beneficial to his constitution.

The young Duke often visited Kensington to stay with his aunt Mary, who especially enjoyed his company while the King was away fighting on campaign in Europe. King William may have been small in stature, asthmatic and prone to dark moods, but for the little Duke this brave and dashing uncle – who was a skilled soldier – was the ultimate role model.

From a very early age the Duke demonstrated a passionate interest in all things military. As well as his two companies of boy soldiers that he drilled in Kensington Gardens, he also had a miniature battleship in his bedroom at Campden House, manned by his playmates who bombarded the 'enemy' with bags of peas. However, his uncle's real life warfare held a particular fascination for the boy and each summer he would trace the King's progress on the European battlefield using maps and charts. He even offered the King his own little regiment to fight in Flanders.

The sudden death of Queen Mary in 1694 meant that the young William's position in the line of Protestant succession grew in importance. Unless

La Maison Royalle d'Angleterr

1. Guillaume 3me. Roy d'Angleterre d'Ecosse et Irlande né le 4. Novembre 1650. 2. Marie Rein
d'Angleterre son epouse est née le 30 Auril 1662. et mourut le 20. Decembre 1694. 3. Georges Princ
Danemarq né le en 16 a epousé en 4. Anne Princesse d'Angleterre 5. Guil
Duc de Glocester leur fils Unique est né le 24. Iuillet 1689.

Above William, Duke of Gloucester by Sir Godfrey Kneller, *c*1699. Dressed in armour, the boy soldier had only a year to live.

Opposite The English royal family, reconfigured by the death of childless Queen Mary. William III sits beneath a portrait of his late wife, with his sister-in-law Princess Anne (later Queen Anne) and William the 'son and heir' resplendent in full wig. Standing next to the King is Anne's husband, Prince George of Denmark.

his uncle remarried and had a child, or his mother Anne produced a healthy baby, he remained the only recognised heir to the Stuart dynasty. As a result, the King became increasingly involved in the Duke's upbringing and education. For his seventh birthday he awarded the boy the Order of the Garter and in 1698 gave him his own household with the Duke of Marlborough as governor and Bishop Burnet as head tutor. Finally, early in 1700 William III moved him into rooms at Kensington Palace that had belonged to Mary, a clear mark of the little Duke's place in the King's affection and a sign that preparations were being made for the boy, one day to succeed as king.

The little Duke's eleventh birthday in July 1700 was a wonderful affair. The royal family celebrated at Windsor with the traditional feasting, bonfires and fireworks. These celebrations were to be short-lived, however, because the next day it became clear that something was wrong. The boy had been exhausted by the festivities and was ailing. The doctors present tried many remedies, including the common practice of bleeding, but none improved his condition. Already frail, the boy continued to weaken and died a few days later.

There was a national outpouring of grief for this last young Protestant Stuart heir – echoing the personal grief of his family. At Kensington Palace, the widowed, childless King was bereft. He told the boy's mother, 'It is so great a loss to me as well as to all England, that it pierces my heart with affliction'.

William died, childless, two years later. The crown passed to his sister-in-law Anne, who died at Kensington in 1714 leaving no direct heir, the last of the Stuart monarchs.

3

A 'very uncouth fellow with a black long wig'

Tsar Peter the Great, Russia's most revered emperor, had an unquenchable thirst for knowledge, scouring Europe to acquire expertise and the latest scientific discoveries. In 1697 King William III gave him a yacht; a shrewd and calculated gift because Peter, unable to restrain his curiosity, abandoned Holland and came to London to play with his new toy.

The trip was to be a sensation for England, but for Peter, it became a huge shopping expedition and what we would today call a 'fact-finding mission' that would have a long-term influence on the history of Russia. In three months, the Tsar toured endless places of interest, visiting the Tower of London, Hampton Court, the opera and music hall, the Royal Mint, Royal Observatory, shipyards and workshops.

Though Peter shunned polite society, preferring instead to drink with his companions in the public houses of Deptford, King William called on him at a merchant's house near the Strand in London. On 23 January 1698, he returned the compliment by coming to Kensington Palace for dinner with the King. The Tsar was shown around the State Apartments, and particularly William's new gallery, which had been completed almost three years before and was a showpiece of new architecture. Peter was drawn not by the paintings or gilded furniture, but by the delightful gadgets he encountered. The anemoscope with its moving dial telling the direction of the wind fascinated him, and on discovering that an ingenious system of strings and pulleys worked the curtains automatically, he drew them again and again with an almost child-like fascination. At the end of an enjoyable evening, William persuaded him to sit for a portrait by Sir Godfrey Kneller.

Not everyone was impressed by the Tsar. William Williams, the under-keeper of the Ashmolean Museum in Oxford, described him as 'a very uncouth fellow with a black long wig and indifferent good coat with gold buttons. His sword hung as if he had never worn one before. He stoop'd much, his hands dirty and scratch'd as if itchy and his face untrim'd, though I could not have a full view of it by reason of the fullness of his ugly wig'. King William did not mind, nor did Kneller, who painted a most flattering image of the 'great sovereign' dressed in the armour of a warrior. That portrait, which still hangs in the Queen's Gallery, is England's enduring souvenir of a truly momentous expedition.

Above A rare survival, this silver medal commemorates the date on which Tsar Peter I of Russia and King William III of England first met on 11 September 1697 in Utrecht, Holland. At over 2 metres tall, Peter would have towered over the diminutive William but here – tactfully – they are given equal stature! The other side of the medal **(below)** shows the distinctive profile of King William III.

Opposite Tsar Peter the Great of Russia, painted during his stay in England by Sir Godfrey Kneller in 1698. When not posing for this flattering portrait or drinking with his friends, Peter was out shopping. He bought vast quantities of books, medical instruments, woodworking tools, models of ships and even a fabulously expensive geographical clock.

EN MARY.
WISS

4

Mary, Queen of China

Above The royal couple, soon to be King William III and Queen Mary II, prepare to leave their Dutch home for a new life in England in 1688.

Opposite Queen Mary II painted by Willem Wissing, between 1686 and 1687 when she was Princess of Orange.

When 15-year-old Princess Mary was told by her father that she was to marry her cousin the Prince of Orange, she wept for a day and a half. William was 12 years older than Mary and several centimetres shorter, added to which he had a slightly hunched back, a hooked nose and suffered chronically from asthma. Marriage to William would mean the teenage girl leaving behind all that was familiar to her and travelling to Holland, her new husband's homeland.

Mary, a handsome brunette, was the eldest surviving daughter of James, Duke of York and his first wife Anne Hyde. Her childhood had already been troubled by the early death of her mother, but her uncle, King Charles II, took a great interest in his niece when it became apparent that his own marriage would be childless. When Anne Hyde died he declared 9-year-old Mary and her little sister Anne 'Children of the State'. They were removed from the custody of their father and brought up under the King's charge as Protestants.

After a sheltered life, and fearing the worst from her impending marriage, Mary decided to take her nanny, her chaplain and her drawing master as company. However, once in Holland she blossomed, finding married life much more agreeable than she had first feared. William's dour exterior concealed a kind and funny personality. He introduced her to his homes – the Binnenhof in The Hague, and Honselersdijk his country retreat – which were comfortably and cheerfully furnished, and which Mary found surprisingly clean after her experience of living at Whitehall Palace in London.

After little more than ten years in Holland, the course of Mary's life was to change once again. On the death of her uncle, her father had succeeded to the throne of Great Britain as King James II. Though initially well liked, his Catholic regime proved so unpopular after just three years that in 1688 William was invited by a group of noble families and politicians to take the throne. His invasion was uncontested. James II, his queen and baby son fled to France. At this turning point in British history, Mary was offered the throne. She refused to reign without her husband, however, so at a ceremony in the Banqueting House in Whitehall in April 1689, Parliament formally offered them both the crown. In a quiet but momentous revolution, the balance of power shifted, and William and Mary were hailed as the first constitutional monarchs, establishing a tradition that endures to the present day.

Royal life actually changed very little. Whitehall Palace, the principle royal home in the capital, remained damp and gloomy, which presented problems for William. The palace was situated on the bank of the Thames, and being so close to the river made his asthma worse.

Almost the first thing the royal couple did was to seek out a new home. They settled on Nottingham House, a fine but modest Jacobean villa in more pleasant surroundings to the north of the city, which they quickly turned into a cosy residence. Sir Christopher Wren, the royal architect, was set to work immediately in what was to be a speedy project, as Mary was anxious to move into their new home. The Queen visited often, impatient to see her project completed, every time giving encouragement.

However, her urging the workmen to work swiftly had disastrous consequences. Vaults were constructed on bad foundations and the walls raised quickly before the soft lime mortar had time to dry and settle, so that in November 1689 part of the new building collapsed, sending scaffolding, timber and masonry crashing into the cellars, together with several of the workmen. One man was killed and others badly injured. Mary had been touring the site just minutes before and was very shaken. For her it must have been a sign, and she wrote to William, 'It pleased God to shew me the uncertainties of things ... for part of the house which was new built fell down ... It shewed me the hand of God plainly in it, and I was truly humbled.'

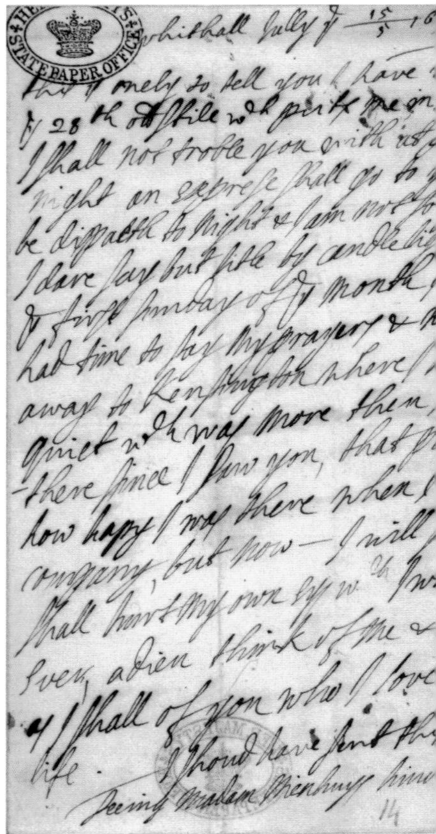

STATE PAPER OFFICE

whithall July y 15/5

this is onely to tell you I have
y 28th of this wch puts me in
I shall not troble you with it
night an expresse shall go to
be dispatch'd tonight & I am
I dare say but little by candle li
y first sunday of y month,
had time to say my prayers &
away to Kensington where I
quiet wch I was more then
there since I saw you, that
how happy I was there when I
company but now — I will
shall have my own
Every adieu think of me &
as I shall of you who I love
life. I should have sent th

Despite this setback, building continued at a pace and on Christmas Eve that year William and Mary were able to move in. Mary was delighted, writing in her memoirs, 'Blessed be the God who has at last after nine months being in England ... brought me to a place where I hope to be more at leisure to serve my maker.'

The real pleasure began when Mary embarked on the task of furnishing her new apartments. The 1690s was a period of immense richness, with luxury goods flooding into Europe from exotic foreign lands, and Mary's taste mirrored the fashion. Her rooms were soon full of Middle Eastern carpets, lacquer screens and cabinets from Japan and rich textiles from India purchased from East India merchants operating in London and Amsterdam.

However, it was Mary's collection of porcelain from China and Japan that dominated every room. When shipments from Asia were opened, the best examples would be selected and reserved to tempt the Queen. We can imagine the chimneypieces stacked up with specially built shelves, crowded with china, set against mirrors to double the effects, or positioned prominently on brackets over doors and on every flat surface in the room. Some had blue decoration on white porcelain; others were brightly coloured. There were figure groups and pieces set in costly

Above An engraving of a china closet by the designer Daniel Marot in 1702. The smaller rooms of the Queen's apartments at Kensington Palace, crammed with Mary's beloved porcelain, probably looked very similar.

Left Despite an unpromising start to married life, Mary came to love William very much. She wrote this affectionate letter to him while he was away fighting in Ireland in 1690, saying that she longed to be at Kensington where: 'I have had hours of quiet ... that place made me think how happy I was there when I had your dear company ... ' and ending with, 'think of me and love me as I shall of you who I love more than my life'.

gilded mounts. Daniel Defoe recorded that Mary's enthusiasm for porcelain immediately set a trend: 'The Queen brought in the fashion ... of filling houses with China-ware which increased to a strange degree afterwards ...'. It was not long before collections had been made and were on display in upper and middle class homes up and down the country as everybody aspired to emulate the queen.

Within these exotic interiors Mary continued to enjoy her domestic pleasures. In her gallery – and extension to her apartments built in 1690 – she had bird cages upholstered in red velvet set up in the windows and velvet beds scattered across the floor for her dogs. Mary was a gifted amateur needlewoman, and had embroidery frames set up so she could work on projects with her ladies in waiting, while one of their company read out loud.

The routine of life continued uninterrupted until Christmas 1694, when Mary, waking one morning, noticed a rash on her arm. She immediately recognised the signs of smallpox, a disease which she had escaped until then, but which had nearly taken the life of her sister Anne, leaving her pock-marked and scarred. Calmly, methodically, this remarkable 32-year-old woman started to prepare for her death. Before telling William the dreadful news she set her affairs in order, sorting out her jewels, writing out instructions for her funeral, listing her debts and burning many private letters.

William, who had seemed cold and undemonstrative to many observers, was distraught. In tears he admitted to Gilbert Burnet, Bishop of Salisbury that 'From being the happiest, he was now going to be the miserablest creature on earth'. The King sent away all members of staff who had not had the disease, and ordered that a camp bed be set up in Mary's bedroom so that he could be constantly at her side, ministering to her tenderly until the end. Despite the best efforts of her doctors, Mary died on 28 December 1694.

And what of her china? It was a perk of the job that the Queen's household would take her possessions, a cold and heartless practice which would see precious objects like beds, clothes and even personal mementoes divided up. All the porcelain was taken by the Duke of Albemarle and shipped off to his home on the Continent, where it was lost over time. Today, just a few pieces remain to remind us of a queen's passion.

5

The room that launched a career

Sometimes a palace could be a theatre, the Court playing out the drama, and the gorgeous rooms with their painted ceilings merely the painted backdrop. This 'scenery' at Kensington was created through intrigue and luck, to launch one of the most important artistic careers of the 18th century.

The old Jacobean heart of Kensington had been rotting for years, and reports prepared in 1718 showed that it needed to be rebuilt. King George I agreed, but its replacement, he insisted, had to be dazzling. Colen Campbell, a Scottish architect of some repute, took up the challenge of sorting the problem out, and work began immediately.

At just about the same time, in Rome, an unlikely friendship had been born between two Englishmen who could not have differed more. One was Richard Boyle, a highly-strung, refined gentleman of enormous wealth who happened to be the Earl of Burlington and an authority on architecture and everything tasteful. The other was William Kent, an outspoken Yorkshireman of humble origins, who was talented, intelligent, artistic and charismatic, in addition to being fond of wine and mutton steaks. In the 18th century, where social position was a major preoccupation, he was that rare creature who could charm his way across the divide. After years spent exploring Italy and devouring art and architecture at the expense of generous patrons, the 'Signor', as he was fondly known, returned to England, and while complaining about the bad wine and cold weather, cast around for something to do.

Above A coronation portrait of George I painted by Sir Godfrey Kneller in 1714. The King immediately embarked on a programme of rebuilding, and then when looking for a painter, was introduced to a decorator with a difference!

Opposite The chubby yet charismatic artist and designer William Kent, painted at the height of his career by Bartholomew Dandridge, *c*1736.

Meanwhile at Kensington, the new rooms had been finished but still needed decorating, and the King's official painter Sir James Thornhill was called for to submit a quote for the largest, the Cupola Room, so-called for its soaring coved ceiling. Thornhill prepared a design and gave a price of £800, before retiring confidently and waiting for the commission. He hadn't reckoned on Burlington, who held many positions of influence and detested Thornhill's politics and his old-fashioned Baroque style of painting. The Vice-Chamberlain Thomas Coke also happened to be one of William Kent's old chums from Italy, and colluded with Burlington, calling in the 'Signor' to give his own quote. A price of £350 was mentioned, perhaps whispered suggestively in his ear, and the King, sensing a bargain, agreed.

We are told that 'a mighty mortification fell on Sir James Thornhill' at the news of this trumping by an upstart, but despite some undignified

Above The ceiling of the Privy Chamber showing Mars and Minerva, god and goddess of war, presiding over the arts and sciences, painted by Kent in 1723.

Opposite The Cupola Room at Kensington Palace, showing Kent's lavish painted decoration of the walls, completed in 1725.

pleading, for him the star of success had waned and fame began to shine instead on the chubby Yorkshireman.

Kent set to work instantly, recreating the coffered ceiling of the Pantheon in Rome, or some would say stealing poor Thornhill's design without a pang of conscience. Within two months, half the decoration was finished, but even as he dabbed away in bronze and gold on the scaffolding, his enemies circled below. A three-man commission of artists, after peering long and hard complained 'tis our opinion that the perspective is not just', noting that they had seen 'very few worse for such a place', but their complaints fell on deaf ears, as Burlington protected his friend and brushed away the critics.

When the room was finished with its painted pilasters, marble chimney-piece and gilded lead statues it must have dazzled in the flickering candlelight, but others called it 'a terrible glaring show'. It would have been a tense moment when King George came to view it, but he liked it.

Over the next few years, Kent painted another six ceilings at Kensington, before finishing with the haunting figures on the King's Stair (see pages 28–29), grudgingly acknowledged by his peers as his best work. The rest, as they say, is history and Kent – his credentials now firmly established – enjoyed immense success until the end of his life. When we look up at the gods and goddesses portrayed in his paintings, we should remember how his fate was in their hands.

6

A wild boy comes to the palace

In 1725, villagers living in the forest near Hanover found a boy all alone in the wild woods. Apparently 11 or 12, he could climb trees with amazing agility, and had been living upon acorns. The villagers tried to take him into captivity; he tried to escape. One account suggests that they sawed down the tree in which he sat before he was finally caught.

Peter the Wild Boy, as he was named, had curly hair, and was outwardly normal, except that a poorly healed wound to his left hand had fused two fingers together. He scampered along, using his arms like a chimp. The strangest thing about him was that he could not talk.

The villagers threw him into the House of Correction, but from here news of his strange, speechless condition rippled out, and reached the ears of King George I at his summer palace of Herrenhausen outside Hanover. He took a fancy to the Wild Boy, made him part of his household, and brought him over to London.

Here, in 1726, the Wild Boy became a wildfire success. Everyone came to Court to see him and his curious ways. Unlike the astonished courtiers, Peter often laughed, refused to bow to the King, and acted with complete abandon. Curious visitors would often find that Peter picked their pockets in search of nuts.

Gradually the King and courtiers tried to tame the Wild Boy. They got him a suit of clothes, though the wearing of them was 'most uneasy' to him. They tried to teach him to use a chamberpot and a bed. And they employed John Arbuthnot, the doctor and satirist, to try to teach him to speak. His progress was slow and painful as he had 'a natural tendency to get away if not held by his coat'.

Today we think that Peter was probably autistic. He never learned to say more than his own name, 'Pe-ter'. Eventually the Kensington Court got bored of him. He was sent to live on a farm near Berkhamsted, where the farmer's family looked after him. Peter lived there to a ripe old age. He was fond of gin and of singing, and in the autumn he would steal away into the woods in search of acorns.

Top Plucked from a feral existence in a forest near Hanover, Peter the Wild Boy became an object of curiosity within the Court of George I.

Below After the Court tired of his antics, Peter went to live with a farmer's family near Berkhamsted, Hertfordshire, until the end of his long life. This is claimed to be his gravestone in the nearby church of St Mary's, Northchurch.

Opposite Peter the the celebrity wild boy. Part of an 18th-century broadsheet about Peter's mysterious early years.

An ENQUIRY HOW THE Wild Youth,

Lately taken in the Woods near *Hanover*, (and now brought over to *England*) could be there left, and by what Creature he could be ſuckled, nurſed, and brought up.

That of this Youth the famous Aſtrologer Mr. *William Lilly* 100 Years ago propheſied, appears by the four other Things which are come to paſs, *viz* —1*ſt*. The *Pope*'s going to *Benevento*. 2*ly*. *Spain*'s breaking the *Aſſiento* Treaty.

3*ly*. The Emperor's ſending the *Oſtend* Company to *China*.

4*ly* The Quality's admiring the new *Italian* Singing Woman lately come over, and really named Signiora *Fauſtina*.

And 5*ly*. This *Wild Youth*, in his following famous Prophecy.

> When Rome ſhall wend (i. e. go) to Benevento,
> And Spaniards break the Aſſiento:
> When Spread Eagle flies to China,
> And Christian Folks adore Fauſtina:
> Then ſhall the Woods be Brought to Bed,
> Of Creature neither taught nor fed,
> Great Feats ſhall he atchieve——

GIven Gratis (for the Satisfaction of the Curious) Up One Pair of Stairs at the *Anodyne Necklace* juſt by the *Fountain* Tavern in the *Strand*: At Mr. *Jer. Payne*'s *Toy-ſhop* in *Pope's Head Ally*, in *Cornhil*. At Mr. *Greg*'s at *Charing Croſs*. And by the Author's Servant *R. Bradſhaw* by *Soho Square*, to be Directed to by LETTER, as in the laſt Page.

I'm Queen Caroline's milliner, so if you want an exquisite hat just ask for Mrs Tempest.
I hope you are admiring my fabulous staircase – another Kent masterpiece.
You must be the Housekeeper judging by the size of those keys!
I am Mohammed, as Keeper of the King's Closet I am his Majesty's most intimate servant!
I, Mustapha, was captured in battle against the Ottoman Empire, but I came to serve King George I as a trusted personal valet.
Pe – ter!

The fabulous painting that adorns the King's Grand Staircase was painted by William Kent in the 1720s, and features the portraits of 45 servants who worked in the royal household. They lean over the balustrades, looking down at you as you make your way up to seek an audience with the King. Here, some of the colourful characters introduce themselves.

DIEU ET
MON DROIT
JOHN LORD HERVEY Lord Privy Seal in the Reign of KING GEORGE

8

'Men, women and Herveys'

Top A medallion portrait by James Thornhill of Queen Caroline, (when Princess of Wales) in the coving of the State Bedchamber at Hampton Court Palace.

Below The corresponding medallion portrait by James Thornhill of George II (when Prince of Wales) in the coving of the Queen's State Bedchamber at Hampton Court Palace.

Opposite Court chronicler and wicked wit Lord John Hervey, holding the purse of office as Lord Privy Seal in this portrait of 1741 by Jean-Baptiste van Loo.

Court life at Kensington Palace under King George I must have been rather forlorn. The King had no wife (he had locked her up in a castle for infidelity) and shunned large formal gatherings. When George II and his wife Caroline succeeded in 1727, the palace came back to life and was often packed with partygoers. During those times a remarkable record was kept by Lord Hervey, a courtier and writer of searing wit who glided through the swirling throng picking up tit-bits, which he diligently recorded in his diary. Lady Mary Wortley Montagu, in her own shrewd assessment, observed that the human family consisted of 'men, women and Herveys'.

Lord Hervey's Memoirs, as they're called, are full of Court intrigue and gossip. There was plenty of it. Although he was the Court's Vice-Chamberlain and so a man of authority, he had many vices of his own. He shared a mistress with Frederick, Prince of Wales and disappeared to Italy with his male lover from time to time. (His beautiful wife Molly, a former maid of Queen Caroline's, was first sad, then bored, and later ran off to France herself.) Above all, Lord Hervey was a brilliant observer and writer who offers us a rare glimpse into the inner workings of the royal Court.

The most important woman in Lord Hervey's life was undoubtedly George II's wife, Queen Caroline. He loved his fat, funny, clever German, who would have preferred to read books instead of making polite drawing room conversation, or to have been discussing philosophy with Sir Isaac Newton. Unlike the King, Caroline had a keen and discerning taste in art, and created at Kensington a 'cabinet of wonders' in which she kept rare and precious specimens from which to learn about the world: a unicorn's horn, a stuffed humming bird, crystals.

Lord Hervey was an antidote to the King, keeping Caroline sane by providing her with 90 minutes of jokes every morning while she had her breakfast (sour cream and fruit). He also took her side in a long-running feud with her son Frederick, the Prince of Wales. Like all the Georgian kings and queens, Caroline and George II maintained bitter relations with their heir, and Kensington Palace was the scene of many noisy rows.

Lord Hervey also sided with Caroline against her husband, and she had much to put up with from the King's fiery temper. He described one typical Kensington morning with George II, who came into the gallery

in a bad mood, and 'snubbed the Queen, who was drinking chocolate, for being always stuffing, the Princess Emily [Amelia] for not hearing him, the Princess Caroline for being grown fat, the Duke for standing awkwardly, Lord Hervey for not knowing what relation the Prince of Sultzbach was to the Elector Palatine'.

In another row with Caroline he berated her for moving the pictures around without his permission. He was particularly annoyed with her for taking his 'Fat Venus', a painting by Vasari, out of the drawing room. (He made her put it back, and he'd be glad to know that it is still in its proper place today.) But these were mere tiffs, to be made up at bedtime. Caroline suffered more seriously from her husband's dreadful infidelities, particularly with one of her very own servants. Henrietta Howard was one of Caroline's 'Women of the Bedchamber', who helped her to get dressed in the morning. Perhaps Henrietta's meek and gentle character made it a little easier for Caroline to tolerate her rival; certainly Henrietta absorbed much of the King's ill temper.

When Henrietta luckily inherited some money, she finally plucked up the courage to leave both the King and the Queen. George II was

Above Giorgio Vasari's *Venus and Cupid*, the so-called 'Fat Venus' that caused a famous altercation between George II and Queen Caroline at Kensington Palace. The painting was based on a cartoon by Michelangelo, whom Vasari much admired and claimed as his tutor.

Opposite The King's 'meek and gentle' mistress Henrietta Howard, who bore the brunt of the King's bad temper. Painting by Charles Jervas, c1724.

glad to see her go, as he'd become bored with his mistress of 20 years, and called her 'an old, dull, deaf, peevish beast'.

Life for the King, Lord Hervey and the court changed forever in 1737, when Caroline fell ill with a dreadful umbilical hernia. Over the horrible nine days until her death, she showed immense bravery and compassion, even finding the time to laugh when her doctor, leaning over her with a candle, set fire to his wig. It is said that George, finally realising what he was about to lose, fell in love with her once again on her deathbed. After this, both the King and Lord Hervey were never quite the same again. Lord Hervey's friends, knowing how much he had loved the Queen, described how the rest of his life was 'not worth thinking of'. For the palace and Court, its glorious heyday was over, and the world of Lord Hervey's Memoirs – cruel, often ugly, but fizzing with passion – came to an end.

9

The old man and the sea

King George II disliked having his picture painted. He sat for the obligatory state portraits, where we see him arrayed in ermine, a crown at his side and a sceptre in one hand, looking every inch a king. These are familiar, but they are more official images than actual likenesses. Informal portraits – those which capture the essence of a person – are much rarer. One man who managed to do just that was Robert Edge Pine. Wanting a different kind of picture, the artist discreetly hid himself away in a closet or cubbyhole at the top of the grand staircase at Kensington where his patience was rewarded, because he eventually spied the King standing quite alone. Sensing his opportunity, the sketchbook was immediately and surreptitiously brought out, and a lightning pencil sketch drawn. The finished painting could be said to portray a shuffling old man of 76, slightly stooped and certainly care-worn, lacking in any of the confidence of those earlier, regal images, when he had been crowned at Westminster Abbey. But it is also a poignant, humble and very human painting, which allows us to get closer to George II than any of the history books.

The story does not end there. Frederick Calvert, Lord Baltimore, the proprietary governor of the English colony of Maryland purchased the painting, intending to give it to the loyal citizens there. A story is told that when the painting was crossing the Atlantic, pirates attacked the ship, and carried off the painting as booty. Later, the pirates themselves were apprehended by the Royal Navy, who, by the law of the sea, seized their possessions as government property and so the painting was taken on the long journey back to England. In 1784 it was bought for 50 guineas by Sir John Griffin Griffin, the owner of Audley End in Essex, where it still hangs in the Dining Room to the present day.

Above The royal yacht, the *Royal Caroline*, built in 1749, painted by John Clevely the elder in 1750. Similar sailing ships that crossed the Atlantic were vulnerable to attack from pirates.

Opposite King George II in 1759; captured first by painter Robert Edge Pine, then later by pirates!

10

The house of oranges

Architects often talk about 'Queen Anne style' just as furniture experts refer to 'Queen Anne legs'. But where can we go to find the definitive Queen Anne style? The answer is the Orangery at Kensington, one of London's most beautiful and perfectly formed buildings. Queen Anne, reigning for such a short time, was not a great builder, preferring instead to improve her gardens. But at Kensington in the summer of 1704 she conceived a new 'greenhouse' with a terrace where she could grow citrus trees and exotic plants in ceramic pots.

Above Queen Anne, painted by Michael Dahl in 1795.

Opposite A Kia-Ora Orange advertisement from 1947, 'In the Orangery'. The beautiful Orangery at Kensington Palace, conceived by Queen Anne in 1704, remains one of her enduring legacies of style.

In theory it should have been a simple job, but building the Orangery turned out to be anything but straightforward. Sir Christopher Wren was by now fairly elderly and probably delegated the work to his assistant, Nicholas Hawksmoor. The Queen approved his design and money was requested immediately from the Treasury, so that the new building 'may be covered in before winter according to her Majesties expectation'. Nobody had reckoned with the young upstart Sir John Vanbrugh who mischievously made a few alterations of his own to the design and managed to wave them under the nose of the Queen. She liked it and ordered the expensive changes, to the horror of the Treasury, who paid the bills and never liked spending money.

Vanbrugh began to stir up other muddy waters. Construction was the responsibility of the Office of Works, a creaking, inefficient government department which was notoriously corrupt. The master-mason Benjamin Jackson was thus perfectly suited. He knew how to milk the system and was probably fiddling his expenses. Vanbrugh hated him; unsuited for the task, he fumed; a villainous fellow and 'scandalous in every part of his character', being 'a very poor wretch; and by many years regular course of morning drunkenness, has made himself a dos'd sott'. Jackson was ordered off site, and a Mr Hill duly employed in his stead. However, a few days later, when Vanbrugh arrived to check on progress, he found no sign of Hill, and after making enquiries discovered that Hill had been visited by heavies 'with some hints of what should befall him if he durst meddle with the master mason's business'.

Jackson was clearly a thug, and we have to wonder if he had some kind of a hold over Sir Christopher Wren, who seemed very relaxed about the whole affair. Hill, said Wren, was 'whimsical and superstitious, and would venture upon nothing till he had consulted the starrs, which

"a very poor wretch; and by many years regular course of morning drunkeness, has made himself a dos'd sott"

— a furious Vanbrugh rubbishes the master mason

Above Sir John Vanbrugh in a portrait by Sir Godfrey Kneller, c1704-10. Vanbrugh won Queen Anne's approval for his embellished designs for the Orangery but found himself at the mercy of the notoriously corrupt Office of Works when it came to hiring a stonemason.

Below The Orangery at Kensington today, a popular venue for delicious afternoon teas and glamorous functions.

probably he had not found favourably enclin'd upon the occasion, and therefore had refus'd the work'. A few days later, a new mason arrived on site, but Vanbrugh soon recognised him as one of Jackson's men. Outwitted by the old foxes, he had no choice but to cave in. The Lords Commissioners of the Treasury probably gasped when they received the final bill for £6,126, almost three times the original estimate! We have to wonder how much found its way into dishonest pockets. But what does it matter now, over 300 years later? Jackson got the job done and the Queen loved the building, hosting parties and even distributing the Maundy money to her deserving subjects, just as the present Queen does every year in the great churches of the land.

These days, the Orangery is still used for parties, or the visitor may sit and drink tea on a sunny afternoon, just as Queen Anne once did three centuries ago, marvelling at Richard Stacey's brickwork and admiring the architecture and the skill of Mr Vanbrugh. Or was it Hawksmoor, or even Wren? We may never know.

11

'I was very much amused...'

Above A pensive 16-year-old Princess Victoria in this self-portrait.

Opposite The Duchess of Kent and her daughter Princess Victoria, by Henry Bone after Sir William Beechey, 1821. The young Victoria holds a miniature portrait of her late father who had died the previous year.

Previous page The King's Grand Staircase at Kensington as it looked when Victoria was born at the palace, by Charles Wild and published in W H Pyne's *The History of the Royal Residences*, 1819.

The little girl who would become one of our most famous and longest reigning monarchs was born at Kensington Palace on 24 May 1819. With the death of her father just eight months later, her widowed mother, the Duchess of Kent, devoted herself to bringing up her daughter in readiness to rule. Daily life for the little princess at the palace included lessons, musical training, riding, visits to the opera and the theatre, but not much companionship of children her own age.

Victoria began a daily 'journal' in 1832 after being given a 'small octavo volume half bound in red morocco, of a very unpretentious kind' by her mother. She continued to write daily, even after she became Queen. These early extracts – in her original spelling and idiosyncratic punctuation – give a glimpse of her girlhood at Kensington.

On Christmas Eve at Kensington Palace in 1832, Victoria and her mother are joined by Sir John Conroy (her mother's physician and advisor), Lehzen, her beloved governess, her Aunt Sophia, her cousin Victoire and her Aunt Mary, The Duchess of Gloucester.

Monday, 24th December — ... *At ¼ to 7 we dined with the whole Conroy family and Mr Hore downstairs, as our Christmas tables were arranged in the dining-room.*
After dinner we went upstairs. I then saw Flora, the dog which Sir John is going to give Mamma. Aunt Sophia came also. We then went into the drawing room near the dining room. After Mamma had rung a bell three times we went in. There were two large round tables on which were placed two trees hung with lights and sugar ornaments. All the presents being placed round the tree. I had one table for myself and the Conroy family had the other together. Lehzen likewise had a little table. Mamma gave me a lovely pink bag which she had worked with a little sachet likewise done by her; a beautiful little opal brooch and earrings, books, some lovely prints, a pink satin dress and a cloak lined with fur. Aunt Sophia gave me a dress which she had worked herself, and Aunt Mary a pair of amethyst earrings. Lehzen a lovely music-book. Victoire a very *pretty white bag worked by herself, and Sir John a silver brush....*
Mamma then took me up into my bedroom with all the ladies. There was my new toilet table with a white muslin cover over pink, and all my silver things standing on it with a fine new looking-glass. I stayed up until ½ past 9....

Victoria had a little pony called Rosy that she adored, and a little dog called Dash, who endured some humiliation at the hands of his royal mistress...

SATURDAY, 13TH APRIL 1833 — ... *I awoke at 7 and got up at 8. At ¼ to 9 we breakfasted.... At 12 we went out riding in the park with Victoire, Lehzen and Sir John. It was a* delightful *ride. We cantered a good deal.* SWEET LITTLE ROSY WENT BEAUTIFULLY!!

TUESDAY, 23RD APRIL — ... *At ¼ past 12 we went out riding with Lady Conroy, Victoire, Lehzen and Sir John. We rode a little way in the park, but the fog was so thick that we turned round and rode down by Gloucester Road and turned up by Phillimore Place, where it was very fine and not at all foggy.... We came home at ½ past 1.... Sir John dined here and I dressed* DEAR SWEET LITTLE DASH *for the second time after dinner in a scarlet jacket and blue trousers....*

FRIDAY, 24TH MAY — ... *To-day is my birthday. I am to-day fourteen years old! How* very old*!! I awoke at ½ past 5 and got up at ½ past 7. I received from Mamma a lovely hyacinth brooch and a china pen tray. From Uncle Leopold* [King of the Belgians] *a very kind letter, also one from Aunt Louisa and sister Feodora.... At ½ past 2 came the Royal Family. The Queen gave me a pair of diamond earrings from the King. She gave me herself a brooch of turquoises and gold in the shape of a bow.... At ½ past 7 we went ... to a Juvenile Ball that was given in honour of my birthday at St James's by the King and Queen. We went into the Closet. Soon after, the doors were opened, and the King leading me went into the ball-room. Madame Bourdin was there as dancing-mistress. Victoire was also there, as well as many other children whom I knew.... I danced with my cousin George Cambridge, then with Prince George Lieven, then with Lord Brook, then with Lord March, then with Lord Athlone, then with Lord Fitzroy Lennox, then with Lord Emlyn. We then went to supper. It was ½ past 11; the King leading me again. I sat between the King and the Queen. We left supper soon. My health was drunk. I then danced one more quadrille with Lord Paget. I danced in all 8 quadrilles. We came home at ½ past 12. I was VERY much amused....*

THURSDAY, 30TH JULY 1835 — ... *at ½ past 11 we went ... to St James's where I was to be confirmed. I felt that my confirmation was one of the most solemn and important events and acts in my life; and I trusted that it might have a salutary effect on my mind. I felt deeply repentant for all what I had done which was wrong and trusted in God Almighty to strengthen my heart and mind.... I was dressed in a white lace dress, with a*

Top Princess Victoria in a self-portrait at around the age of 13.

Above An early drawing by the young princess, taken from her first sketchbook.

Opposite A contemplative young Victoria captured in this drawing of 1829 by Richard James who was later appointed royal lithographer by the Queen in 1837.

Above The Duchess of Kent with Princess Victoria by Sir George Hayter.

white crape [sic] *bonnet with a wreath of white roses round it.... The whole was performed by the Archbishop, who also read a fine address to me composed by him expressly for the occasion. He did the whole very well, and I felt the whole* very deeply....

Sunday, 23rd August — ... *After dinner I took up Mrs Butler's Journal* and read a little in it.... One would imagine by the style that the authoress must be very pert, and not well bred; for there are so many vulgar expressions in it. It is a great pity that a person endowed with so much talent as Mrs. Butler really is, should turn it to so little account and publish a book with is so full of trash and nonsense which can only do her harm....*

*Fanny Butler, née Kemble was a popular actress who wrote an 'indiscreet' journal in 1835, which achieved considerable success!

Above Originally a gift to the Duchess of Kent, the cocker spaniel, Dash, became a much beloved companion to the young princess.

Opposite A portrait of Princess Victoria by Sir George Hayter.

Tuesday, 25th August — ... *At ½ past 2 sat to M. Collen for my picture til 1.2 past 3, while Lehzen read to me in Mme de Sévigné's Letters. How truly elegant and natural her style is!... Then I played on the piano. At 4 we walked out with Lady Flora and Lehzen.... In our walk we met a man with beautiful parrots. Amongst them one was dear little paroquet of a green colour with a pale brown head and so very tame that Mamma took it on her finger and it would hardly leave her. It talks, also, the man says.... Mamma bought the dear little thing. It is now in Mamma's room....*

Tuesday, 20th June 1837 — ... *I was awoke at 6 o'clock by Mamma, who told me that the Archbishop of Canterbury and Lord Conyngham were here, and they wished to see me. I got out of bed and went into my sitting room (only in my dressing-gown), and saw them. Lord Conyngham (the Lord Chamberlain) then acquainted me that my poor Uncle, the King, was no more and had expired at 12 minutes p. 2 this morning, and consequently that I am* Queen.

When Victoria met Albert

VICTORIA FIRST CAUGHT SIGHT OF ALBERT AND HIS BROTHER ERNEST WHEN THEY ARRIVED AT KENSINGTON PALACE ON 18TH MAY, 1836, ACCOMPANIED BY THEIR FATHER ERNEST, DUKE OF SAXE-COBURG-GOTHA

VICTORIA WAS DELIGHTED WHEN HER UNCLE PRESENTED HER WITH A TAME PARROT

OVER THE NEXT FEW DAYS, THE COUSINS SPENT MUCH TIME TOGETHER...

I like my Cousins extremely,
they are so kind, so good,
and so merry...

I sat between my dear
Cousins on the sofa and
we looked at drawings.
They both draw well,
particularly Albert.

VICTORIA'S MOTHER THE DUCHESS OF KENT GAVE A BALL AT KENSINGTON AND ALBERT AND VICTORIA DANCED UNTIL THREE IN THE MORNING

THE NEXT DAY

ON FRIDAY 10TH JUNE, VICTORIA SAID GOODBYE TO HER FAMILY

I embraced both my dearest Cousins most warmly, as also my dear Uncle. I cried bitterly, very bitterly

VICTORIA AND ALBERT EXCHANGED LETTERS OVER THE NEXT FEW YEARS, DURING WHICH TIME VICTORIA WAS CROWNED QUEEN. WHEN THEY MET AGAIN IN 1839, VICTORIA HAD TO TAKE THE INITIATIVE AND PROPOSE, AS SHE FEARED THAT ALBERT WOULD NEVER DARE NOW THAT SHE WAS QUEEN. SHE AND ALBERT HAD NINE CHILDREN AND LIVED HAPPILY TOGETHER UNTIL HIS DEATH FROM TYPHOID IN 1861. VICTORIA WAS HEARTBROKEN AND MOURNED HIM UNTIL HER DEATH IN 1901.

12

The bookworm, the artist and the party princess

The elegant, spacious apartment to the south side of Kensington Palace has been home to three very different members of the royal family. In passing, there seems to be little to link a book-mad duke, a sad artist and a jet-setting princess apart from the fact that they called Kensington Palace home. Though they belonged to different generations and different centuries, each life was lived out in the same rooms, in a part of the palace we call today Apartment 1a. On closer inspection, these royal lives – unusual, unconventional and tinged with sadness and frustration – share striking similarities.

When Kensington Palace fell out of favour as a royal residence in 1760, its many rooms were broken up into discrete apartments to accommodate a succession of dukes, princesses and courtiers. In the largest apartment (though it was even larger in the past) lived George III's sixth son, Augustus, Duke of Sussex (1773–1843), then later Queen Victoria's fourth daughter Princess Louise (1848–1939) and most recently HM Queen Elizabeth's sister, Princess Margaret (1930–2002).

The private lives of all three were often turbulent. The Duke of Sussex was one of the most popular of George III's wayward sons but his youthful romance and marriage to Lady Augusta Murray in Rome in 1792 was deeply disapproved of by his father, who declared it illegal under the Royal Marriages Act of 1772. The Duke was forced to give up Lady Augusta, but not until she had borne him two children. Nor did the act stop him contravening it again some 38 years later, when he married Lady Cecilia Buggin, a meek and mild-mannered lady who would not have hurt a fly. For Princess Louise, marriage allowed her to escape the fate of playing constant companion to her widowed mother and she was the first child of a monarch to be married (legally) to a commoner since 1515. However, her husband was no man in the street, but John, Marquess of Lorne, heir to the dukedom of Argyll, a nervous and restless aristocrat, whose relationship with Louise was often strained. Long periods of separation fuelled rumours of fulfilment outside the marriage, although in later years the couple developed a companionable friendship; when he died in 1914, Louise was bereft. Princess Margaret's highly romantic love affair with the dashing but unsuitable Peter Townsend in the 1950s courted much public controversy, not least as Margaret was the younger sister of the newly crowned Queen. Her tempestuous marriage to the

H.R.H. PRINCESS LOUISE SCULP
VICTORIA R.
1837

Above Princess Margaret in Apartment 1a in 1988.

Opposite The iconic statue of Queen Victoria in her coronation robes on the West Front, designed by her daughter Princess Louise and unveiled in 1893 to celebrate Victoria's Golden Jubilee.

hip young photographer, Antony Armstrong-Jones (later Lord Snowdon), with affairs on both sides, continued to excite a sense of scandal, and despite the birth of two children the marriage finally ended in a bitter divorce.

These royal residents of what became Apartment 1a also struggled in their search for a meaningful position in public life. Such has been the common dilemma of 'lesser' royals through the centuries. Frustrated by his father's refusal to find him a fulfilling role, the Duke of Sussex further alienated himself from his family with his liberal political views and support for causes such as Catholic emancipation and parliamentary reform. Princess Louise displayed an obvious creative talent, which she was allowed to develop to become an accomplished artist. During her time at Kensington a studio was built for her in the palace grounds and here she created the famous statue of her mother that stands in Kensington Gardens. Her artistic practice, coupled with her support for causes such as the women's movement and non-denominational education, demonstrated an individuality that marked her apart from the traditional concerns of her mother's court. Louise also had the common touch. Years later she would go shopping alone in Kensington High Street, and even ride the trams, to the horror of King George V. 'What', he is said to have exclaimed, 'would grand-mamma have thought!'

For Princess Margaret the move from adored daughter of a king to sister of a monarch left her without a clearly defined role. Although she regularly carried out public engagements, especially for her many charities like the Royal Ballet and Dr Barnardo's, it was usually the exotic lifestyle at her Mustique holiday home and the size of her civil list allowance that caught the attention of the press.

Augustus, Louise and Margaret were all noted for their artistic interests and were avid collectors, of people and objects! The Duke of Sussex amassed a vast and wide-ranging library of over 50,000 volumes, housed at Kensington in specially-made mahogany bookshelves that eventually took over much of his living quarters. Princess Louise's wide circle of artistic, bohemian friends included her tutor the sculptor Ernest Boehm, the composer Arthur Sullivan and the artist Frederic Leighton. During the 1960s, when Apartment 1a was home to Princess Margaret and Lord Snowdon, it became famous for gatherings of A-list celebrities.

While there was much about these three mavericks that bucked traditional royal trends, none of them ever forgot their exalted position. In the end, perhaps the most striking similarity between these three was the constant conflict they faced between their public duty and private passions.

Previous page (from left to right) the 'bookworm' Augustus Duke of Sussex by Guy Head (detail), 1798; 'the artist' Princess Louise, photographed in about 1860; and 'the party princess' Princess Margaret, photographed by Cecil Beaton in 1958 in front of a portrait of her by Pietro Annigoni

13

Kensington at war

In 1940 the Blitz raged over the skies of London as the Luftwaffe attempted to carry out Hitler's threat to destroy London. Kensington Palace did not escape the onslaught unscathed; on the night of 4 October it suffered a direct hit. Struck by a firebomb, designed to scatter and ignite inflammable materials, the roof of the palace erupted into flames, and for a few hours firefighters battled to save the building from complete destruction.

By the beginning of the war, change had already come to Kensington. Almost imperceptibly, the old order was giving way to the new. Princess Louise had died just three months after its outbreak, and Princess Beatrice, covering her furniture with dustsheets and 'closing up house', moved to more tranquil surroundings in the country to sit it out. She never returned, dying in 1944. Most of the other residents had also moved to their country houses to escape the Blitz. A few were abroad, including the Earl of Athlone, who spent the war as Governor-General of Canada.

German Heinkel bombers over London in 1940 during the Blitz. Kensington Palace was not spared from the bombs that rained down on London night after night and suffered a direct hit.

His wife the Countess was better known as Princess Alice of Athlone, a lively and interesting character who lived to a great age. She died in 1981, the last survivor of Queen Victoria's 40-odd grandchildren.

On that fateful October night the only person about was a caretaker who was looking after the Athlones' rooms at Apartment 4. His name is not recorded, although he is mentioned in several letters as heroically removing unexploded bombs from the palace and somehow escaping injury as the bombs fell around him. Lady Bertha Dawkins, a lady-in-waiting to Queen Mary, lived in a small apartment overlooking Princesses Court. She wrote a letter to Queen Mary about the incident. 'Your Majesty has heard, I believe of the incendiary bombs on Kensington Palace on Monday night. We went up yesterday to see my ruined house … only two rooms of the State Apartments have been damaged and nothing much hurt inside.'

This was an understatement of the situation, as the State Apartments were quite badly affected, with the Queen's Drawing Room, a 17th-century panelled room, suffering extensive damage. Thankfully, the fire had not spread to any of the great treasures or the painted ceilings nearby.

Lady Bertha, however, didn't spare the Queen the details of the damage to her own rooms: '… my bedroom is wrecked by fire and water, all my Victorian mahogany furniture badly burnt. Water drips everywhere, ruining each room downstairs as well.'

The morning after: daylight reveals the extent of the 1940 bomb damage to the north range of Clock Court and adjoining parts of the Queen's Apartments. The Athlones' apartment is to the left of the partially burnt roof. The State Apartments were reopened to the public in 1949; shortage of materials after the war meant that some parts of the palace were not repaired until the 1980s.

The area next to the damaged Queen's Drawing Room formed part of a small suite of rooms, known as Apartment 5, which were lived in by Sir Derek Keppel and his wife. Sir Derek was a direct descendant of Arnold Joost van Keppel, one of King William III's closest confidants, who had also lived at the palace. The raid that night shattered the apartment and rendered their home 'only a shell and quite uninhabitable'.

The Athlones' home was probably the worst hit. They had left the place fully furnished and adorned with many souvenirs from their trips abroad – big game trophies, paintings, carpets from Aleppo and lamps from Cairo. They had also spent money on refurbishment, installing electricity and creating a new bathroom. By the morning after the raid, the scene was chaotic. A friend took charge of salvaging what they could and described it for Queen Mary. 'I am sorry to say that the new bathroom is completely gutted … There is a great deal of debris, of course, as that end is burnt through.' The damage could have been much worse as they went on to recount that, 'I understand that the Caretaker moved five incendiary bombs from the step of Clock House [Lord Althlone's apartment] on the night following the bomb which did so much damage … I am thankful to say that no lives were lost, and that there were no injuries. We cabled Lord Athlone to assure him on this

point and to give an account of the damage.'

In 1946 on the Athlones' return from Canada they found their apartment still uninhabitable, so went to stay with Queen Mary at Marlborough House until it was put back in order. In her *Reminiscences*, their daughter Princess Alice wrote, 'Kensington Palace was quite uninhabitable … Our apartments there were in complete chaos. The disastrous fire had destroyed part of our roof and attic rooms… No window frames were left, and all our furniture, books and pictures were heaped higgledy-piggledy in the drawing room and dining rooms … Aunt May [Queen Mary] even came to help wash china … It was all very annoying, but we laughed a lot over our tasks.'

By the end of the war, a bankrupted and bombed nation was in no mood to spend money repairing royal palaces, and the King himself ordered that no money was to be allotted to Kensington while Londoners remained homeless. It was not until June 1949 that the State Apartments were opened to the public again, and only in the 1980s was the last of the war damage finally made good.

14

Party palace

'Saturday night last was a great entertynment made for the Prince of Baden at Kensington, where was dancing and gaming, and a great supper: and banquets of sweetmeats ... there could not be less than 1,000 persons, but it was 5 of the clock in the morning before some of them could get home.'

Kensington has long had a reputation for entertaining, with some parties wilder than others! The era of magnificent balls began with its earliest royal inhabitants, William and Mary. The party described by London bookseller Richard Lapthorne (and re-created here!) in January 1694 was one of the last in a three-year golden period beginning in 1691, when the King and Queen held at least 14 magnificent social events at the palace. The ornate rooms, elegant staircases and impressive halls, lit by extra candles and lanterns, rang with laughter, chatter and music as the royal couple, conscious of the need to reinforce their status and eager to show off the newly-finished palace, held fashionable balls, with dancing literally until dawn.

A wide variety of food and drink was laid on to provide sustenance for the guests who, when not dancing, could amuse themselves by gambling or card playing, supported by liberal quantities of beer, ale, mead, cider, port and other wines, while the kitchens worked full time to provide bread, fruit, meat and fish. For the delight of diners, fantastic displays of confectionery and sweetmeats were presented in triumph – on one occasion this took the form of a 'square Piramede of the best Confeccons'.

A large number of staff was needed for such lavish affairs and often extra servants were brought in from St James's Palace, their travelling expenses carefully recorded and reimbursements paid. To ensure that the courtiers had a safe journey home, Susanna Becker, a servant was supplied with oil to keep the lamps by Hyde Park burning all night.

When his beloved Mary died in 1694 William lost his enthusiasm for these grand entertainments and instead held more sedate musical evenings and concerts. Queen Anne presided over a more exciting social scene, with ceremonies revived, and the Orangery was constructed with an eye to providing a large and flexible space for entertaining.

King George I's parties at Kensington after 1714 were, however, a very different sort of affair. The King was not a naturally sociable man and he tried to avoid dancing and lively parties. When advised that he needed to keep the favour of the court, he started Sunday gatherings, which became known as 'Drawing Rooms'. These were held in the King's Gallery after his morning visit to the Chapel, with the aim of meeting 'society'.

In theory everyone was welcome to attend a Drawing Room; in reality only those who could afford suitable court attire were allowed inside. Two gentleman ushers stood guard at the outer doors and, if the visitor was not fit for the eyes of the King, the guards' halberds would clash together and prevent entry. Some courtiers spent a fortune on expensive new clothes, although arriving with a favourite of the King would smooth the way. Failing all else, a couple of silver shillings slipped quietly into receptive hands might do the trick.

Once inside, everybody stood in the King's presence, sometimes for hours, and conversation was conducted entirely in French. From our modern perspective, we can see why George I may not have enjoyed this, but he tried his best. However, his courtiers weren't fooled. Privately, they mocked his forced civility, his wooden conversation and crude German manners, while bowing and scraping to his face, all the while maneouvring for his social approval and favour. If the King was seen to speak with you, your social standing rose by several notches. However, if you were snubbed and the King turned his back, your popularity would plummet.

On the King's 43rd birthday in 1718, his usual Drawing Room was followed by an afternoon and evening garden party, which is well recorded. A William Byrd, a rich planter from Virginia was visiting London at the time. He tells us: 'I dressed me very fine to go to Kensington [it] being the King's birthday, and about 2 went to Sir Wilfred Lawson's and we went together and found a great crowd in the Gallery, where the King saw company. People were not very fine', Byrd sniped in his diary. However, the crush of people in the gallery shows how important it was to be seen supporting the King and, like Byrd, to be seen celebrating his birthday. Later that evening things started looking up. 'About 10 o'clock the fireworks were fired and were very fine. The little princesses danced till 11.'

Almost 200 years later, the year 1905 saw what must be classed as the last great party at the palace. Princess Victoria Eugenie Julia – known as Ena – the daughter of Princess Beatrice, turned 18 and, as she had come of age, was formally introduced to society. 'Coming out' followed a long-established tradition, with a formal presentation to King Edward VII

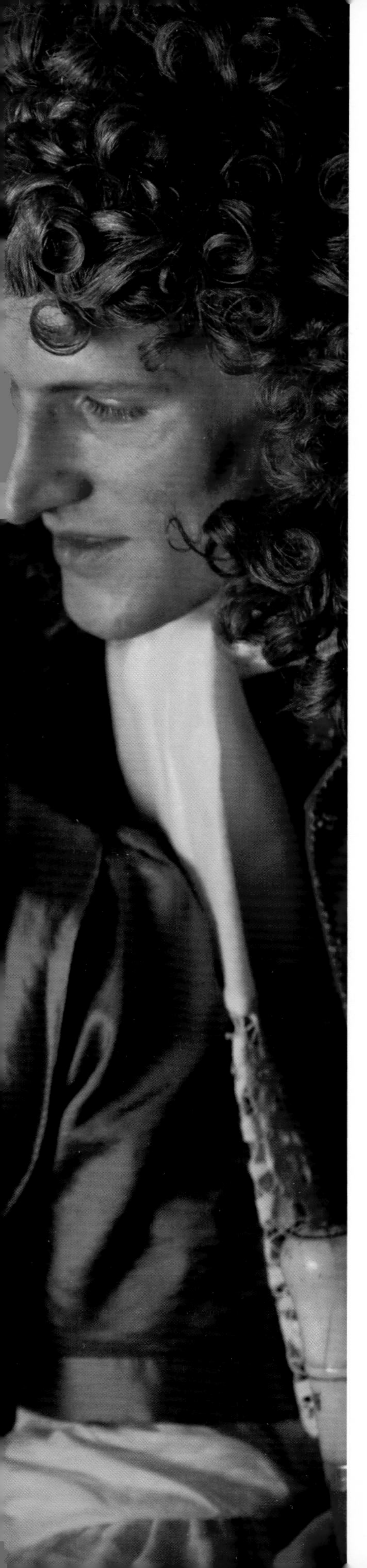

at Buckingham Palace, followed by a flurry of society balls, presentations and entertainments in a seemingly endless sequence.

Ena's own ball at Kensington was 'the first dance there in the memory of anyone living' and, as she was very popular with the public, the papers scurried to report every detail. Several members of the Royal Family attended, including the King. The *Star* proclaimed that 'she laughed with everybody at everything, declining altogether to be formal'.

A stellar array of royalty and other guests used the grand King's Staircase to make their entrance as dramatic as possible, and took refreshment in the Red Saloon where Ena's grandmother Queen Victoria had held her very first council meeting almost 70 years before. Princess Ena's lively smile and relaxed manners charmed the guests. One young man who rather formally and stiffly asked the Princess for a dance was gently teased with the words, 'Oh, are you sure you don't mind?'

Great things were planned for Ena, who as Queen Victoria's granddaughter was one of the most eligible brides in Europe. The following year she met King Alfonso XIII of Spain, and fell in love. In a rare break with tradition, she was permitted to convert to Catholicism, and so became Queen of Spain, leaving Kensington forever. Yet her life was not to have a happy ending. Ena carried a silent, sinister gift from Queen Victoria in the form of the haemophilia gene, which she passed on to her son. In 1931 as her adopted kingdom disintegrated into civil war, she left for exile in Lausanne, Switzerland – the Kensington fairytale a distant memory.

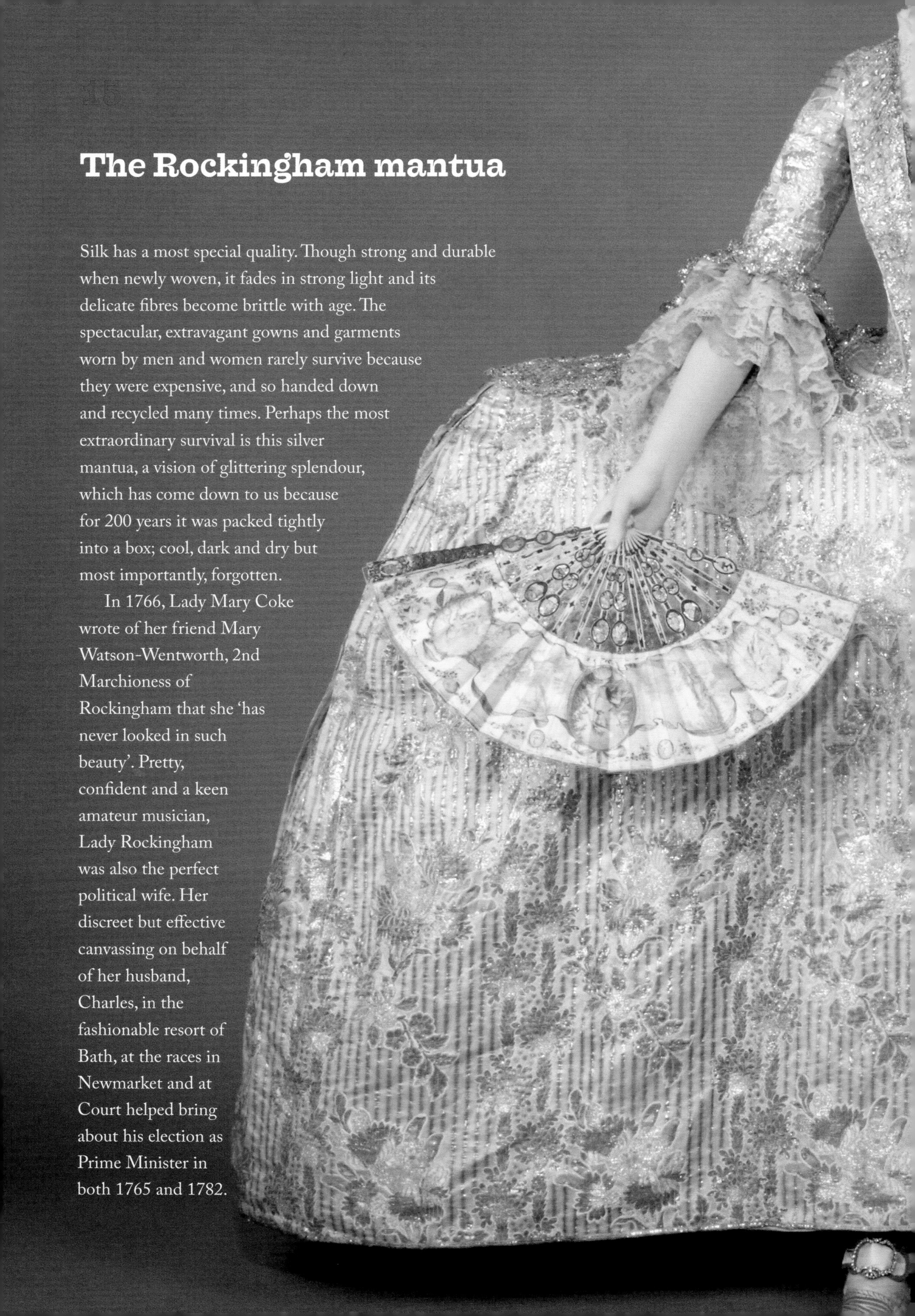

15

The Rockingham mantua

Silk has a most special quality. Though strong and durable when newly woven, it fades in strong light and its delicate fibres become brittle with age. The spectacular, extravagant gowns and garments worn by men and women rarely survive because they were expensive, and so handed down and recycled many times. Perhaps the most extraordinary survival is this silver mantua, a vision of glittering splendour, which has come down to us because for 200 years it was packed tightly into a box; cool, dark and dry but most importantly, forgotten.

In 1766, Lady Mary Coke wrote of her friend Mary Watson-Wentworth, 2nd Marchioness of Rockingham that she 'has never looked in such beauty'. Pretty, confident and a keen amateur musician, Lady Rockingham was also the perfect political wife. Her discreet but effective canvassing on behalf of her husband, Charles, in the fashionable resort of Bath, at the races in Newmarket and at Court helped bring about his election as Prime Minister in both 1765 and 1782.

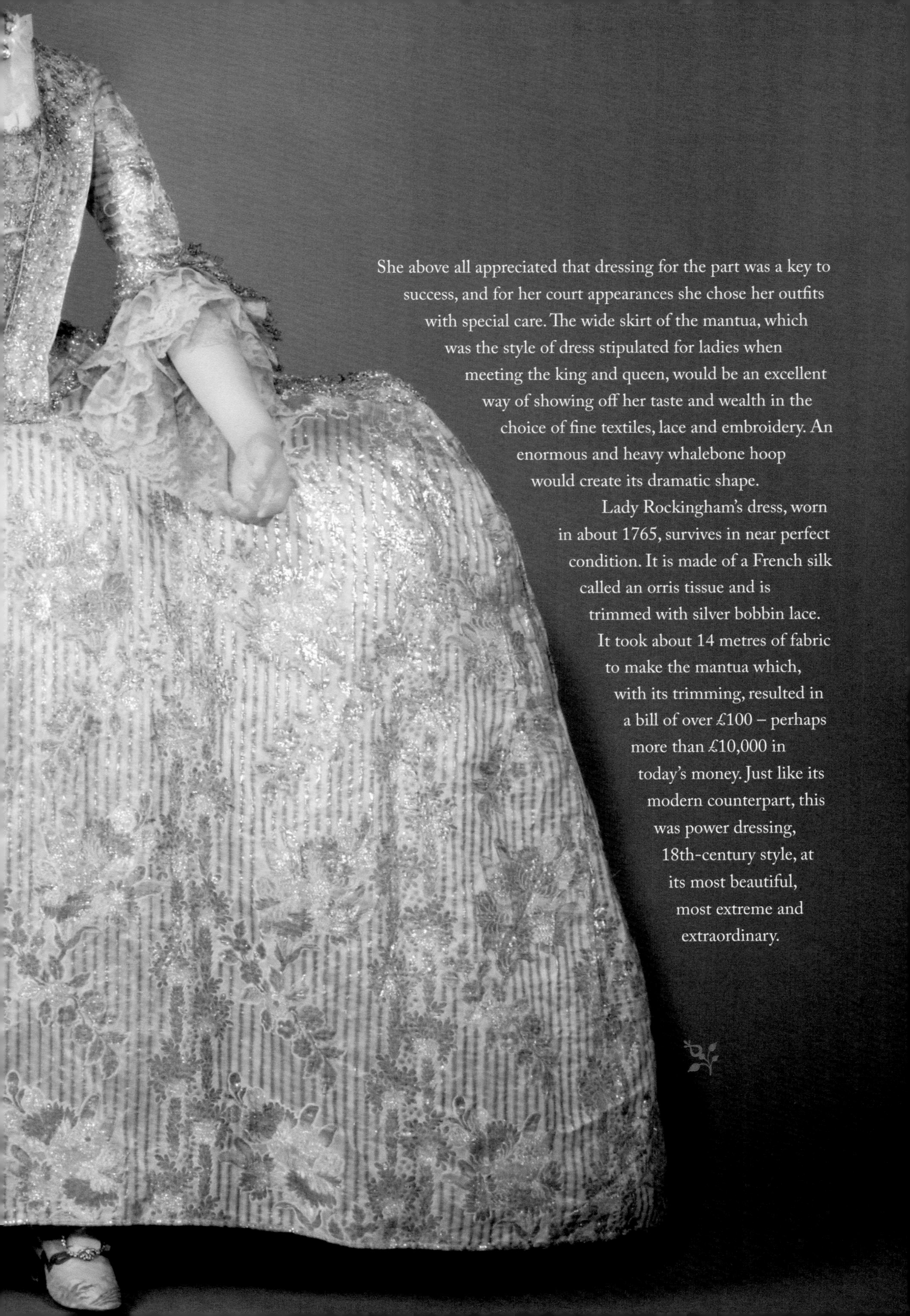

She above all appreciated that dressing for the part was a key to success, and for her court appearances she chose her outfits with special care. The wide skirt of the mantua, which was the style of dress stipulated for ladies when meeting the king and queen, would be an excellent way of showing off her taste and wealth in the choice of fine textiles, lace and embroidery. An enormous and heavy whalebone hoop would create its dramatic shape.

Lady Rockingham's dress, worn in about 1765, survives in near perfect condition. It is made of a French silk called an orris tissue and is trimmed with silver bobbin lace. It took about 14 metres of fabric to make the mantua which, with its trimming, resulted in a bill of over £100 – perhaps more than £10,000 in today's money. Just like its modern counterpart, this was power dressing, 18th-century style, at its most beautiful, most extreme and extraordinary.

MEET THE BEATLES!
The First Album by England's Phenomenal Pop Combo
Capitol
HIGH FIDELITY

ow (l-r) A young aret in a Paris tclub; the Beatles' US album, 1964; ol couple Snowdon d Margaret at the *Help!* m premiere, 1965.

Middle row (l-r) Dancing at the Georgian Ball, Mansion House, 1964; Margaret photographed by Snowdon.

Bottom row (l-r) The Rolling Stones; Margaret and close friend Peter Sellers in London's Soho; the Princess on her 29th birthday photographed by her future husband.

16

Kensington's coolest couple

After their marriage in 1960, Princess Margaret and Lord Snowdon moved into Apartment 1a at Kensington Palace in 1963. The couple became the darlings of Swinging London, counting 60s icons Mary Quant, Vidal Sassoon, Liz Taylor and the Beatles among their circle. The cool royal couple were markedly different from previous generations of the royal family. The Princess, wearing a headscarf and sunglasses, would ride astride Lord Snowdon's motorcycle as they visited street markets and bargained for quirky antique furniture on Portobello Road. For longer trips, they drove a Mini or an Aston Martin. They went to jazz clubs, avant-garde films and loved the theatre.

The couple's celebrity connections grew in part through Snowdon's photography contacts. Snowdon had worked for Tatler magazine, Vogue, The Sunday Times and many others. By the close of the decade he had photographed virtually everyone who was anyone in the arts world, including Alec Guinness, Christian Dior, Sophia Loren, Noël Coward, Tom Stoppard, Margot Fonteyn and Rudolph Nureyev, Marlene Dietrich, and Francis Bacon.

The couple first encountered the Beatles in 1963 at the Prince of Wales theatre in London. It was on this occasion that John Lennon made his famous remark, 'on this next number I want you all to join in. Would those in the cheap seats clap their hands. The rest of you can rattle your jewellery.' A few months later, the Princess and Lord Snowdon attended the premiere of the Beatles' first film, *A Hard Day's Night* – and got to know them better at the private party afterwards. John Lennon affectionately nicknamed the Princess 'Priceless Margarine'.

Comedy actor Peter Sellers and his wife, Swedish actress Britt Ekland, were particularly close to the royal couple. They spent weekends together at Royal Lodge, Windsor, and would often go round one to another's homes for dinner parties. One evening at Kensington Palace, at a gathering organised by Margaret to celebrate her sister the Queen's 39th birthday, there was a showing of a home movie. The film was shot by Snowdon, directed by Tatler's publisher Jocelyn Stevens, and starred Sellers, Ekland, Snowdon and Margaret herself. Packed with antics, the film ends with the Princess, Snowdon and Sellers high-kicking in a chorus line!

Apartment 1a, Kensington Palace was the perfect party venue for entertaining such famous friends. Just a short drive from London's West End and the chic addresses of Mayfair, the apartment reflected Margaret and Snowdon's artistic flair and eclectic tastes. Guests would arrive via the stylish entrance hall, with its chequered slate and marble floor and modern 18th century-style architectural details, created by Lord Snowdon and his friend, the theatre designer Carl Toms. They would be greeted by the most modern-looking of royals: the Princess, in dramatic eye makeup, a fashionable bouffant hairstyle, perhaps wearing a Dior dress with low décolletage, and Snowdon wearing a dinner jacket with a simple white silk polo neck.

A dozen or so people would enjoy a lively dinner round the oval mahogany table in the royal couple's striking coral-coloured dining room, decorated with paintings by John Piper. The subdued lighting – the couple never used overhead lights – created a cosy atmosphere, drinks would flow generously and each guest in true 60s style, would have his or her own personal ashtray. On other occasions, a glittering crowd would stay in the blue and grey drawing room until the early hours of the morning. Spike Milligan, of the 'Goon Show', and the songwriter Richard Stilgoe would play off each other; John Betjeman, the future poet laureate, would tell stories.

Sometimes, party guests would join in as the Princess played show tunes on the black baby grand piano in her drawing room, singing numbers from *Showboat*, *Guys and Dolls* and *South Pacific*. Friends noted her incredible memory for lyrics. Noël Coward recalled these evenings at Kensington as 'charming', remarking in his diary, 'Princess Margaret was surprisingly good. She has an impeccable ear, her piano playing is simple but has perfect rhythm, and her method of singing is really very funny.'

Top row (l-r) Margaret meets Marilyn Monroe and other stars; playwright Noël Coward and filmstar Marlene Dietrich; the Goons Peter Sellers, Spike Milligan and Harry Secombe.

Middle row (l-r) 'Priceless Margarine' meets the Beatles in 1963; Mick Jagger and then girlfrien Marianne Faithful in 196

Bottom row (l-r) Marg meets James Bond st Sean Connery and his wife Diane Cilento in 1 the Princess with F Sinatra at a charity concert; time to p period-style!

17

The day the King of Greece came to call

Below stairs in a royal palace, another life existed – that of an army of servants who kept the building running and the residents comfortable and well-fed. Like a scene from 'Upstairs, Downstairs', everyone knew his or her place, but service brought with it inclusion in a wider family, and a refuge from ordinary life.

In 1938, at the age of just 14, young Joan Cook was pulled out of school by her father, put on a bus in faraway Sunderland and waved off on the long journey to London to go into service. 'I think it was my step-mother', she recounts. 'She and I didn't agree, and she arranged that I would be sent out of her sight.' For Joan, who had never been more than three miles from her home village, London lay at the end of the world, and going there was a terrifying prospect. After an uncomfortable twelve-hour journey, she arrived at Kensington, where she found the shutters closed, and the cold stone floors echoing and unfriendly. By six o'clock the following morning, she was set to work as the assistant cook, though 'kitchen maid would be a better title' as she herself says, to the Dowager Marchioness of Milford Haven.

Above Joan Cook poses outside the sunken garden just after she arrived at Kensington in 1938 and again **(opposite)** when she returned in 2007, invited back to the palace to record her story.

Her Ladyship, as she was called, was actually a relic of another era, born Princess Victoria of Hesse, whose sister had been the Tsarina Alexandra of Russia. But those great days were gone, the empress fallen and murdered in revolution, and the Marchioness, now widowed and in reduced circumstances, lived in one of the smaller apartments in Kensington Palace. Joan was part of a staff of just four. In her new uniform, she helped to stoke up the fire to provide hot water in the morning for her Ladyship's bath, carrying water in the copper, helping cook prepare the staff breakfasts, and at times undertaking less pleasant tasks like peeling potatoes and plucking and gutting pheasants.

It wasn't all bad, and there were moments of excitement. The dowager lay at the centre of a family web of European royalty, who all came to call. Among the many visitors were Lord Mountbatten, who would be the last Viceroy of India, and Lady Mountbatten, various dukes, princes and even on occasion the odd king or two. Sometimes the servants would hide and peer through the staircase balustrade as the guests prepared to go out and one of these occasions she remembers well.

'Lady Mountbatten was very flamboyant', she says. 'I always remember this emerald-green shining dress. Princess Marina was in a

plain white gown with a tiara'. There were other notable guests – Queen Elizabeth with two little princesses, and Joan can still remember one chastising the other, 'Don't run Margaret, pull your socks up'. Queen Mary sometimes came for tea, when cook would prepare wonderful petit fours and tiny cakes. Others came for longer – including the Dowager's teenage grandson, a young and handsome Greek prince called Philip.

One occasion sticks out in Joan's mind more than others. 'A lot of people would come and call out of courtesy, though we rarely saw them.' One afternoon everybody was out, but after lunch the doorbell rang. 'I wasn't supposed to answer it', Joan remembers, 'but it kept ringing'. She finally plucked up courage, went through the pantry and opened the door. 'There was this huge dark-haired fellow standing there, beautifully dressed. I must have stood there with my mouth open because he said "King George of Greece", and gave me his calling card. I was so shocked I never answered him. I just took the card and he turned round, bowed and walked out.'

'I must have stood there with my mouth open because he said "King George of Greece", and gave me his calling card.'

Joan left Kensington in 1940. When the war broke out, her father called her back to Sunderland. In 1947 her old friends invited her back to help prepare for the marriage of that young Greek prince to Princess Elizabeth, but Joan had just started a new job in her home town. 'In those days work was very hard to get. I asked for leave, and was told that my job wouldn't be there when I got back from London, so I didn't go.'

Opposite King George II of Greece photographed in 1937.

It was almost 70 years before she returned to Kensington, but she has few regrets. 'It's fate', she says. 'I believe your life is mapped out'. Walking on the echoing stones again, memories come flooding back – skating on the pond, trips to the cinema, and walking back from the shops with Princess Louise of Battenberg, who later became Queen Louise of Sweden. 'I was never homesick,' she says. And her Ladyship, what kind of person was she? 'She once took me for a walk in the garden, and that was, I think, the only time when I was ever really talking to her on my own. She took me round the garden and told me what all the flowers were, and every time I see a certain flower I think of that bit of the garden at Kensington'.

For Joan, what she remembers most about the palace is the smell of evening primrose, and a brief, unforgettable encounter with the gentlemanly King of Greece.

18

Kensington in tears

Above When the well-regarded Duke died on 21 April 1843, many thousands of people flocked to Kensington Palace to pay their respects.

Opposite Augustus Frederick, Duke of Sussex, painted by Guy Head, 1798.

Queues of mourners waiting to pay their respects, a daylight funeral, weeping crowds lining the streets of London…

So strong is the link in the public imagination between Diana, Princess of Wales and Kensington Palace that you may be forgiven for assuming that this is a description of the aftermath of her death in August 1997. However, this was not the first time the palace witnessed a huge outpouring of public grief on the death of a member of the royal family.

When George III's sixth son, the Duke of Sussex died at Kensington on 21 April 1843, crowds flocked to the palace in their thousands to pay their respects to this well-loved, easy-going man. Long queues of men, women and children waited patiently at the palace to file past his body in respect. Augustus was an unlikely character to be a popular hero. Though quiet and reserved, he had been dutiful and built up a good public reputation in stark contrast to his siblings, who were dissolute in their personal morals and a financial burden on the nation. Instead, Augustus epitomised a new respectability which people yearned for, which would blossom under his niece, the young Queen Victoria.

Augustus was already elderly in 1843. The death of the young Diana, Princess of Wales came as a terrible shock to a world grown used to seeing her face constantly in the media. In marked contrast to the respectable distance kept between the people and the 19th-century royal family, millions had become fascinated by this attractive young woman, who had metamorphosed from shy teenager to poised princess and devoted mother of the two princes William and Harry. Diana was as famous for her compassion as her celebrity lifestyle; her death released a wave of public emotion.

On the announcement of her death after her fatal car crash in Paris, crowds immediately began to gather at Kensington Palace, adding bunches of flowers, soft toys or other mementoes to an ever-growing mountain of tributes. Soon the golden gates in front of the palace were swamped by a field of flowers, in some places waist-deep.

For two weeks members of the public filed through the palace to sign condolence books; and for the first week Kensington Palace stayed open 24 hours a day to cope with the vast numbers of visitors. An estimated 140,000 people wrote messages expressing their grief.

When the Duke of Sussex died his body lay in state for one day at Kensington Palace and the public were invited to pay their respects.

From 10 in the morning until 6 at night, over 25,000 people made their way through the palace, past specially erected barriers around the body and then left down a wooden staircase built for the purpose out of a second-floor window. The Duke's piper and devoted Burmese page were among those attending his coffin.

Sussex's was the first royal funeral to take place in daylight and over 2,000 police lined the streets to control the crowds. Shops were closed in Kensington and mourning bunting hung along the roads, in scenes echoed 150 years later as crowds lined the streets to pay their respects, flinging flowers onto the limousine carrying her body to its final resting place.

Augustus was not buried in a royal vault. The Duke made a special request to be buried in Kensal Green Cemetery in north London, so that his non-royal wife could be buried next to him. The *Illustrated London News* reported that, 'He is the first of a royal race who has chosen to lay his bones in one of the cemeteries of the people – as if he desired to have his memory identified with them even in death.'

Diana, Princess of Wales was also buried in an usual location for a member of the royal family. Her body lies on an island on a lake at Althorp, her Northamptonshire family home. The connection felt between the public and the 'People's Princess' still remains strong. To this day flowers and messages are left on the golden gates on her birthday and the anniversary of her death.

Above The death of Diana, Princess of Wales, in Paris in August 1997 triggered an outpouring of public grief. Crowds gathered around the palace to lay tributes outside the gates transforming the surrounding area into a sea of flowers.

Opposite Fashion photographer Mario Testino at the opening of a major exhibition of his portraits of the Princess of Wales, held at Kensington Palace in November 2005.

'It is with feelings of regret that I shall bid adieu for ever … to this my birth-place, where I have been born and bred, and to which I am really attached.'

— Queen Victoria says farewell to Kensington Palace in 1837

Four more palaces to explore; hundreds of stories to discover

Hampton Court Palace

Explore Henry VIII's magnificent palace, then stroll through the elegant Baroque apartments and glorious formal gardens of William III and Mary II. Feel the heat of the vast Tudor Kitchens and the eerie chill of the Haunted Gallery, before you disappear into the fiendish Maze...

Banqueting House

Walk in the footsteps of a dazzling company of courtiers who once danced, drank and partied beneath Rubens's magnificent painted ceiling. This revolutionary building was created for Court entertainments, but is probably most famous for the execution of Charles I in 1649. Spare him a thought as you gaze up at this ravishing painting - one of his last sights on earth...

Kew Palace and Queen Charlotte's Cottage

Step into this tiny doll's house of a palace and experience the joys and sorrows of King George III and his family through a soundscape and displays of fascinating personal artefacts. Stroll to Queen Charlotte's Cottage, built in 1770, where the royal family enjoyed picnics and peace in a tranquil corner of Kew Gardens.

Open April - October. Entry to Kew Gardens is required to visit Kew Palace and Queen Charlotte's Cottage.

Tower of London

Gaze up at the massive White Tower, tiptoe through a king's medieval bedchamber and marvel at the Crown Jewels. Meet the Yeoman Warders with bloody tales to tell; stand where famous heads rolled and prisoners wept. Then discover even more surprising stories about the Tower!

We offer an exciting programme of events and exhibitions throughout the year. For more information and details on tickets, group bookings and access for all the palaces please call 0844 482 7777 or visit www.hrp.org.uk

Historic Royal Palaces

Historic Royal Palaces is the independent charity that looks after the Tower of London, Hampton Court Palace, the Banqueting House, Kensington Palace and Kew Palace. We help everyone explore the story of how monarchs and people have shaped society in some of the greatest palaces ever built. We receive no funding from the Government or the Crown so we depend on the support of our visitors, members, donors, volunteers and sponsors.

Supporting us

Our donors, sponsors and members share our passion for history, spectacle and majesty and many of our most ambitious projects would not have been accomplished without their generosity and participation.

Historic Royal Palaces' fundraising campaign finances a number of bold and ambitious projects and will bring the palaces, their treasures and their stories to the widest possible audience. Our campaign is open to everyone. It will ensure the success of a wealth of exciting and ambitious projects and will allow them to be completed sooner than would otherwise be possible. Kensington Palace is the home of a number of such projects, including 'Welcome to Kensington – a palace for everyone', our ambitious programme to bring this palace's stories to life in new and innovative ways.

Please call the Development Team on 020 3166 6321 or email development@hrp.org.uk for more information.

Membership makes a difference

There has never been a better time to join our Historic Royal family! Membership is fantastic value for money. Membership allows you to explore and discover so much more about each of the five palaces with limitless visiting throughout the year. Your subscription also helps us continue to tell the stories and care for these amazing palaces.

To enquire about becoming a member of Historic Royal Palaces and for more information on the range of benefits you receive, please visit www.hrp.org.uk or call 0844 482 7778.

Acknowledgements

Published by Historic Royal Palaces
Hampton Court Palace
Surrey, KT8 9AU

ISBN 978-1873993163

Written by Margaret Dorman (story 18); Rhiannon Goddard (stories 13 and 14); Alexandra Kim (stories 2, 12 and 18); Joanna Marschner (stories 4 and 15); Deirdre Murphy (story 16); Lee Prosser (stories 1,3,5,9,10 and 17) and Lucy Worsley (stories 6 and 8). Extracts in 'I was very much amused...' (page 42) taken from *The Girlhood of Queen Victoria* edited by Viscount Esher and first published by John Murray, London 1912.

'When Victoria met Albert' (page 48) by Margaret Dorman, illustrated by Bill Bragg.

'Party palace' (page 62) photographed by Forster and Forster, and re-created by Past Pleasures Ltd.

Cover illustration and family tree (inside back cover) by Joe McLaren.

Edited by Sarah Kilby and Lee Prosser
Designed by Steve Burgess
Picture research by Annie Heron
Printed by Beacon Press

Further reading

Courtiers *– The Secret History of Kensington Palace*
Lucy Worsley,
Faber & Faber, 2010

Diana, Fashion and Style
Beatrice Behlen and Joanna Marschner,
Jarrold Publishing in association with Historic Royal Palaces, 2007

Kensington Palace *– The Official Illustrated History*
Edward Impey,
Merrell in association with Historic Royal Palaces, 2003

The Royal Palaces of London
David Souden with Brett Dolman and Lucy Worsley,
Merrell in association with Historic Royal Palaces, 2008

For children

Palace Princesses
Elizabeth Newbery,
Historic Royal Palaces, 2010

Historic Royal Palaces is a registered charity (no 1068852)

www.hrp.org.uk